Sure Do Wish You'd Get Ye One of These Here Taters

An Essay on Cormac McCarthy's *Suttree*

WILLIAM GILLESPIE

SPINELESS BOOKS | URBANA, IL

All that night cats moaned in the dark like cats (143)

The policeman's face bore a constant look of tolerant interest. Set the sack down son and let's see what all you got there.

Harrogate rolled the sack from his shoulder and lowered it to the paving and spread the drawstring open with his thumbs. A musky smell rose. He tilted it slightly policeward. The officer thumbed his cap back on his head and bent to see. A prefiguration of the pit. Vouchsafed a crokersack vision of hell's floor deep with the hairy damned screaming mute and toothy toward the far and heedless city of God. He raised his head and looked at the waiting Harrogate and he looked at the bright sky above Knoxville and he turned to the driver.

You know what he's got in that sack? (215)

Sure Do Wish You'd Get Ye One of These Here Taters

An Essay on Cormac McCarthy's *Suttree*

This is an essay about *Suttree*. The first half of this essay is an analysis of the narration in *Suttree*. This analysis attempts to pin down the point of view. The second half of the essay is dedicated to answering the question of why *Suttree* makes me cry. By the end of its first half, the essay concludes that the concept "narrator" is a paradigm that does not apply to *Suttree*. The second half of the essay tries to move from analysis to intuition in the hope of finding an alternative paradigm to "narrator." The essay begins by stating constraints and premises. The constraints are a list of topics this essay will not discuss. The premises are my (at times tentative) understanding of what happens in the novel.

Here are the constraints. This is not an essay about *Suttree*'s author Cormac McCarthy. This essay does not deal with evidence that *Suttree* is autobiographical. This essay is not concerned with other novels by Cormac McCarthy. This essay is also not concerned with any other texts that *Suttree* echoes, including the Bible. This essay is not interested in the distinction between modern and postmodern and will not return to this point. This is not a dismissal—these constraints are regrettable. These topics all shed light on the novel and are all worthy of other essays. However, this essay is not concerned with anything outside the novel except me. One of the things that impresses me about the novel is that I love it. Love is idiosyncratic. Thus the reasons I love *Suttree* are situated not within the novel but within me, and, furthermore, within me this slow spring of 1997. For this reason, this essay is written in the first person and the second half is as indulgent as the first half is precise.

Here are my premises. These premises are my conclusions regarding confusing aspects of the novel. When possible, I provide page numbers that correspond to the evidence from which these conclusions are drawn. My pagination refers to the First Vintage International Edition (May, 1992), although other editions may have identical pagination. Cornelius "Buddy" Suttree is an unambitious (on 68 he shows no interest in adjusting to the demands of the marketplace, on 222 he disposes of extremely effective bait because he can't stand its smell) fisherman of unknown age (my guess is late 20's or early 30's) who lives in a houseboat. He has one (living) brother — Carl (17)— and at least two sisters (130, 421). His parents are living and he avoids all contact with them (on 299 he throws away a letter from his father without reading it). He was raised Catholic (251, 253). He also avoids contact with his wife and child, whom he abandoned. In 1950, Suttree is arrested as an accomplice in a pharmacy robbery (321). He serves a (ten-or-so-month) sentence in the workhouse and is released in January 1951. (The fact that Suttree's charges are revealed to the (alert) reader 220 pages after he has finished serving his sentence should indicate the level of ambiguity that renders this summary necessary.) When Suttree is released, he buys a houseboat, is given two fishing lines strung in the Tennessee River, and lives a hand-to-mouth existence selling catfish and carp, sometimes drum or gar (199). He is college educated (47). He has a reputation for being smart (366), but the only evidence of this is we see that he knows what "yeggs" means (235). (Whether any of the verbose narration can be attributed to Suttree is a question I will return to.) His father's side of the family, which he detests, is wealthy and powerful. His mother's side, for which he has some fleeting sympathy, is generally lower-middle-class and inclined toward alcoholism. The novel and the story begin on a summer Sunday in 1951 Knoxville, about six months after Suttree is released from the workhouse. By defining the chronology of the novel this way, I am also defining pages 30–62 as a flashback to a previous time (as well as a leap to a different place and point of view). This flashback spans about four months and ends near January 1, 1951. Page 63 is the Monday following the Sunday described on 8 through 29. When Suttree, on page 70, addresses J-Bone, Boneyard, and Hoghead with "You sons of bitches havent been to bed," this indicates that the three have been drinking continuously for the 20 or so hours that have elapsed since page 22, having gone through at least two bottles of whiskey before beginning the awful night of drinking that ends with Suttree hungover in jail. The rest of my premises regarding chronology, point of view, and location are less uncertain. They are included as appendices.

I have chosen to study the narration of *Suttree* because the narration creates three contradictions. The first contradiction is between the language of the narration and that of the characters. I assume this contradiction is apparent to anyone who makes it as far as page 12. My second epigraph is an excellent example of what I mean. My second epigraph, if read carefully, also reveals a less obvious contradiction between types of language within the narration. The description of the dead bats is different than the description of the policeman. This essay will return to this point at the end of its first half. The second apparent contradiction is between the narration and the story. Again, a lexically lush and grammatically complex narration narrates a bleak, desolate, and fairly uninteresting story. It is not that Suttree is an uninteresting character, it's even worse. Suttree is an uninteresting character and this is the least interesting period of his life. This is the part Suttree would skip when telling the story of his life: how he went to prison then lay drunk on the river for four years in the transition between abandoning his family and abandoning his home town. The story has an archaic, mythic quality, yet the characters are neither noble nor heroic. None of the characters seem to have any consequence on the world outside Knoxville. Nor do they have much consequence within the novel: it has no plot. It is a series of overlapping anecdotes, most of which do not affect the anecdotes that follow. I find a third contradiction between the first 277 pages of the book and the last 196 pages. The first half of the novel is structurally complex and features Gene

Harrogate as a central character. In the first 277 pages, the point of view passes between Gene and Suttree. The manner in which the point of view is transferred is complex in that sometimes a shift from one point of view to another may also indicate a shift backward in time. This is the case on pages 30, 107, 269, and 274. This transfer, although confusing, is consistent in that the point of view is almost entirely limited to those two characters. In the second half of the book, Gene ceases to be a central character, and there are no chronologic regressions. The point of view is Gene's only twice, and time moves only forward. In one respect, these two "halves" of the book actually are halves — they each span about 23 months, although the first 23 months last 80 more pages than the second 23 months. Unlike the first two contradictions, this third contradiction is a contradiction within the narration, not a contradiction between the narration and another aspect of the book.

A conventional understanding of narration assumes a single narrator who is a human presence as consistent as—although perhaps on a different diagetic level from—the characters. (The difference in "diagetic levels" is the difference between being a character in the story and telling it.) Although conventional narrators are frequently not characters, they tend to have consistent relationships to the characters and events in the story. The narrator is oriented to the story in a particular way and this does not change. Henceforth I will refer to this relationship or orientation as narrative "distance." Three ways narrative distance manifests itself are tense, person, and access to information. A story in the past tense indicates that the narrator is referring back to it from a future point and thus knows how it will end. The narrative distance in this case is greater than the distance between a narrator and a story in the present tense. A first-person narrator is frequently a character in the story. In this case the narrative distance between narrator and story is less than the distance between a third-person narrator and a story. Access to information refers to the narrator's ability to know information characters do not. Such information can include the thoughts of one or more characters (including motivations that the characters themselves are unaware of), future events, and events taking place undetected elsewhere in the setting. When the narrators are characters in the story, frequently they have access to their own thoughts but not those of other characters. For the purposes of this essay, a narrator with a greater degree of omniscience is considered to be more distant from the story than a less omniscient narrator (the farther away you are the more you can see).

None of these three aspects of narration — tense, person, and access — remain consistent in *Suttree*. The narrative distance oscillates in these respects and others. The concept "narrator" does not apply well here. It is difficult to accept the narration as coming from a character in the story or as omniscient. This oscillation is not obvious when reading the novel because so much else remains consistent. Because the narration follows Suttree almost exclusively through time from past to future with occasional jumps forward, the fact that it shifts between past and present tense is not jarring. Because most of the scenes center around Suttree, the manner in which it leaps in and out of his head is not confusing. The majority of the book is written as if by an invisible observer to Suttree's actions. However, the narration occasionally discloses information Suttree does not have access to. There are scenes without Suttree. There is one scene at the beginning (30) from the point of view of a character Suttree does not meet until 435 pages and five years later (465). Occasionally the narration will lapse into the first or second person, as if representing a character's thoughts or addressing a character or both. At one point the narration reveals knowledge of the future — events to come within the story and even well after.

This essay will next list moments of inconsistency in tense, person, and access.

The narration is almost entirely past-tense. However, it has a tendency to slide into present tense throughout the book. This does not mean that the story suddenly leaps from the past to the present. The verb tense typically changes to present for one or two events in the middle of a sequence of past events. The distance between the narration and the story shrinks at these moments. This tense shift functions as a sort of narrative zoom lens — the distance only appears to get smaller. Many, but not all, of these lapses into present tense can be accounted for by a particular (favored) sentence construction using "must." Here are four examples:

> He came up with the pig holding it about the waist, the bucket against the side of his face and blood running all down the front of him, hugging while it kicked and shat. Coming up the creek walking spraddlelegged and half staggering until finally he must stop to rest. He and the pig sitting in the kudzu quietly getting their strength back like a pair of spent degenerates. (139)

"Finally he had to stop to rest" would make more sense.

> In the morning he set out with them. A light heart and deep rejoicing for the fortune of it made the load less heavy yet he must still rest here and there by the streetside. By such stages he labored out Central Avenue small and bowed and wildlooking.
>
> What you got in the sack son? (215)

Quite similarly, "yet he had to still rest" would be more consistent.

> Suttree sat beneath the picture. Jones was standing almost in the middle of the little room and he seemed suddenly mindless, a great towering zombie that she must take by one elbow and steer to the table although he has been here before. She's sewn him up like a hound with carpetthread and the blood beading very fine and bright from the pursings of black flesh, stanching lesser holes with cataplasms of cobweb, binding him in bedlinen. With him drunk at the door two days later demanding to be undone and sewn looser because he could not bend. Eyes raddled with blood, reeking of splo whiskey. (280)

Again, "had to take him by one elbow" would be more consistent, and likewise "She'd sewn him up..." Notice how, in this example, a previous event is described with the present perfect tense ("She's") and a subsequent event is described with the past tense ("could") (He could not bend because she has sewn him up like a hound).

> The old woman's slow hands sorted a loose packet of brown faded photographs, glasses riding down the bridge of her nose as she nods in recognition. She must set them back again with her finger, shuffling these imaged bits of cardboard, paper, tin. They have a burnt look to them, as if dried in a flue. Dark and haggard eyes peer out. (127)

In this example, the "must" sentence functions as a bridge into the present tense. The subsequent sentences continue in the present as the narrative zoom lens zooms in on the photo album. These sentences would be consistent if they went "They had a burnt look to them" and "peered out." There are other examples of this "must" formation as well (102, 383). I assume that these instances of present tense are due to a preference for "must." This novel has other consistent style quirks as well — its own grammar. For example, the comparative "like some," and the use of "nor" without "neither." There are examples of lapses into the present tense, however, without using "must":

> Suttree turned his face up to the night. The snowflakes came dodging out of the blackness beyond the lamps to settle on his lashes. Snow falling on Knoxville, sifting down over McAnally, hiding the rents in the roofing, draping the sashwork, frosting the coalpiles in the crabbed dooryards. It has covered up the blood and dirt and claggy sleech in gutterways and laid white lattice on the sewer grates. And snow has made cool bowers in the blackened honeysuckle and it has hid the packingcrates in the hobo jungles and wrought enormous pastry rings of trucktires there. Where the creek addles along gorged with offal. Upon whose surface the flakes impinge softly and are gone. Suttree turning up his collar. (403)

"It has covered" is present perfect. It would have been consistent with the past tense to use past perfect: "It had covered." The effect of this shift in tense is a diminishing of the narrative distance — it is as if this 1954 snowfall were happening now. The snowfall is given immediacy. It becomes more vivid. Another, clearer example of an illogical shift into present tense can be found in the following:

> Until he blew her a kiss and hunched his shoulders to say that he was cold and went up the steps.

> Now at noon each day he wakes to the gray light leaking in past the gray rags of lace at the window and the sound of country music seeping through the waterstained and flowered walls. Walls decked with random flattened roaches in little corollas of oilstain, some framed with the print of a shoesole.

In the rooms the few tenants huddle over the radiators, flogging them with mophandles, cooking ladles. They hiss sullenly. The cold licks at the window. In the bathrobe and slippers she has bought for him and carrying his pigskin shavingcase he goes along the corridor like a ghost through ruins, nodding at times to chance farmboys or old recluses with skittish eyes emerging from assignations in the rooms he passes. To the bathroom at the end of the hall that no one used save him… (397)

The shift back into past tense is subtle. The moment of return is the choice of "used" over "uses." Because the passage is describing a sequence of events in order, they retain their sequence and seem to remain in the past even though the tense shifts into present. However, what purpose does the shift here serve? In this passage, as in the last, the distance is shortened. We are momentarily drawn into the monotony of these days. The present tense suggests that these days may continue for ever. The past tense would have suggested that they ended long ago. There are other lapses into present tense on 254, 351 and 381.

Suttree's narration also contains inexplicable shifts in person. As with the shifts in tense, certain examples of the shifts in person can be attributed to a particular style quirk — using "you" instead of "he." Here are two examples:

He passed the car almost every day going to and from town. It sat in the front row of Ben Clarks' lot and it looked vicious and barbaric and feline crouched there among the family sedans. These warm days they had the top down and leaning on the wooden sill you could hang your head over the cockpit and drink in a heady smell of rich leather and admire the cluster of black dial faces in the dashboard like an aircraft and the fine red carpeting to match the hide of the seats and the polished

burl walnut and the silver jaguar's head snarling from the
center of the steeringwheel. (405)

It would be consistent with third person to instead say "he could
hang his head…" or even "one could hang one's head." As with the
shifts into present tense, this shift into second person does not
seem terribly odd. It also reduces the narrative distance and makes
the car more seductive, as if we, as readers, could smell the leather.

Suttree rubbed his eyes.

We all got to go sometime.

He looked at the old man.

I said we all got to go sometime. You get older you think about
it. Young feller like you.

The old man gestured in the air with his hand, you couldn't tell
what it meant. (194)

In this example, the "you," technically, should only be "he
[Suttree] couldn't tell what it meant." This is a fairly innocuous
transgression of person, however. It happens again on 62, and 346.
A much stranger example is the opening. Who is addressing whom
in the following?:

Dear friend now in the dusty clockless hours of the town
when the streets lie black and steaming in the wake of the
watertrucks and now when the drunk and the homeless have
washed up in the lee of walls in alleys or abandoned lots and
cats go forth highshouldered and lean in the grim perimeters
about, now in these sootblacked brick or cobbled corridors
where lightwire shadows make a gothic harp of cellar doors no

soul shall walk save you. (3)

This opening cannot be easily assimilated into the rest of the story. While it has a density prevalent throughout the narration, it is not narrating the story. Because it is set in italics it is visually distinct from the text. The only other italicized passage is in the voice of a radio preacher (133–4). Aside from the shared italics, there is no other reason to believe that the opening passage is the voice of a radio preacher. The opening does not refer to any of the characters in the third person, and there is little to indicate that either the first or second person is meant to be one of the characters. Furthermore, while gorgeous, it is a misleading introduction. Its urgent eloquence sets the reader up for a dramatic suspense and terror-driven plot. It is hardly clear upon one's first reading that the opening is describing Knoxville 1951. Why the novel opens in the second person can be best explained by assuming that a narrator is addressing us (dear friend). Similarly, the novel ends in the second person: "Fly them." (471) While ambiguous, this sentence is imperative, with an implied subject of "you." More than the second person connect the opening and closing. They both refer to the huntsman.

> Or a hunter with hounds or do bone horses draw his deadcart through the streets and does he call his trade to each? (5)

The first-person opening and closing frame the novel and can perhaps be considered outside it.

> Somewhere in the gray wood by the river is the huntsman and in the brooming corn and in the castellated press of cities. His work lies all wheres and his hounds tire not. I have seen them in a dream, slaverous and wild and their eyes crazed with ravening for souls in this world. Fly them. (471)

The use of first person in this closing is even more troubling. The fact of the first person in the narration strongly implies the existence of a "narrator." It does not seem to be Suttree's thought, even though elsewhere in the novel first-person sentences do seem to be a transcript of Suttree's thoughts as he thinks about himself. Here are three examples:

> Far clouds rimlit. A brimstone light. Are there dragons in the wings of the world? The rain was falling harder, falling past him toward the river. Steep rain leaning in the lamplight, across the clock's face. Hard weather, says the old man. So may it be. Wrap me in the weathers of the earth, I will be hard and hard. My face will turn rain like the stones. (29)

It is clear that the following passage is from Suttree's point of view as he is dragged out of a roadhouse drunk. The final sentences are Suttree's thoughts:

> His feet went banging down some stairs. He closed his eyes. They went through cinders and dirt, his heels gathering small windrows of trash. A dim world receded above his upturned shoes, shapes of skewed shacks erupted bluely in the niggard lamplight. The rusting carcass of an automobile passed slowly on his right. Dim scenes pooling in the summer light, wan inkwash of junks tilting against a paper sky, rorschach boatmen poling mutely over a mooncobbled sea. He lay with his head on the moldy upholstery of an old carseat among packingcrates and broken shoes and suncrazed rubber toys in the dark. Something warm was running on his chest. He put up a hand. I am bleeding. Unto my death. (79)

Other examples of Suttree's thoughts are no less overwrought:

> He sat with his back to the tree and watched the storm move

on over the city. Am I a monster, are there monsters in me? (366)

At other moments, second-person sentences seem to also be narration of Suttree thinking to himself.

> A clear night over south Knoxville. The lights of the bridge bobbed in the river among the small and darkly cobbled isomers of distant constellations. Tilting back in his chair he framed questions for the quaking ovoid of lamplight on the ceiling to pose for him:
>
> Supposing there be any soul to listen and you died tonight?
>
> They'd listen to my death.
>
> No final words?
>
> Last words are only words. (414)

The narration also demonstrates access to Suttree's thoughts, but in the third person:

> All night he'd try to see the child' s face in his mind but he could not. (150)

Lastly, there are passages where the narration seems to relate Suttree's thoughts as he refers to himself in first, second, and third person:

> He turned heavily on the cot and put one eye to a space in the rough board wall....
>
> In my father's last letter he said that the world is run by those

willing to take the responsibility for the running of it. If it
is life that you are missing I can tell you where to find it. In
the law courts, in business, in government. There is nothing
occurring in the streets. Nothing but a dumbshow composed
of the helpless and the impotent. (13–14)

The first person would appear to refer to Suttree in the first
sentence of the second paragraph, and Suttree's father for the
remainder of the paragraph. From the first person, Suttree's
father addresses Suttree in the third person. If we assume that the
transcript of the letter is being thought by Suttree, this assumption
makes the drift less confusing but also implies that Suttree has a
very good memory.

A paragraph later *Suttree* slides from third to first to second
person:

Suttree turned and lay staring at the ceiling, touching a like
mark on his own left temple gently with his fingertips. The
ordinary of the second son. Mirror image. Gauche carbon. He
lives in Woodlawn, whatever be left of the child with whom
you shared your mother's belly. He neither spoke nor saw nor
does he now. Perhaps his skull held seawater. Born dead and
witless both or a terratoma grisly in form. No, for we are like
to the last hair. I followed him into this world, me. (14)

With "with whom you [Suttree] shared your mother's belly,"
either Suttree is having an internal dialogue, or the narrator is
addressing him and, in his thoughts, Suttree replies. If the narrator
is a presence other than Suttree addressing Suttree, and knows the
name of the cemetery Suttree's stillborn brother is buried in, then
either the narrator knows everything Suttree does or knows things
Suttree does not. There is reason to believe that Suttree does not
know his stillborn brother is buried in Woodlawn. His family kept

the fact of the brother a secret from him (17–18). On the other hand, we have some reason to believe Suttree does know where his stillborn brother is buried — he wakes up in Woodlawn cemetery:

> A maudlin madman stumbled among the stones in search of a friend long dead who lives here. (302)

Most important, only an omniscient narrator would know the name of the cemetery. If Suttree really thinks this way, then perhaps much of the narration can be attributed to him. And Suttree is supposed to be educated, so perhaps "isomers" is part of his vocabulary. But Suttree doesn't speak eloquently, never writes, and he reads books only once in the entire novel (358) (despite frequently lying in bed awake during daylight hours) He does, however, read newspapers (169, 401, 403, 404) and magazines (386). Furthermore, there are enough moments when the narrator has access to information that Suttree does not, for it to be clear that some of the narration cannot possibly be Suttree's thoughts. If the narration has access to Suttree's consciousness, then the absence of certain information is conspicuous. We don't learn what he was charged with until 321, and we don't learn he has a wife and child until 148. Finally, some examples of a shift in person cannot be explained by movements in and out of Suttree's consciousness, such as drift in scenes Suttree is not in:

> He paused at some trash in a corner where a warfarined rat writhed. Small beast so preoccupied with the bad news in his belly. It must have been something you ate. Harrogate crouched on his heels and watched with interest. (100)

Is this third sentence thought (or said) by Harrogate as he contemplates the poisoned rat? The narration is capable of accessing Gene's thoughts, as is clear from 437. If the verbosity of the narration is somehow a reflection of Suttree's thoughts, then why is it present in scenes that Suttree is not in? Even if Suttree knows the word "warfarined," it is far less likely that Gene (who does not have a reputation for being smart) does.

The narration of *Suttree* occasionally demonstrates access to information none of the characters can know, such as events that happen in the future:

> Holmes had shot a dentist in Vestal not long before this and not long after he shot and killed a man across a cardtable at Ab Franklin's and was sent to the penitentiary. Years later he got out and went back to Franklin's and was shot dead himself over the same table. (374)

By the time the death of Holmes takes place, the novel is long over, and Suttree has left Knoxville, presumably forever. Another example of narration accessing information Suttree is unlikely to have is the passage with Dr. Neal. Does Suttree know that the Lawyer's pants fell down in the cafeteria line, or that he was "alone and friendless in a hundred courts?" This passage also indicates that narrative distance oscillates in ways other than shifts in tense, person, and access—for example the way characters are referred to. Suttree addresses Dr. Neal as "Dr. Neal" at the same time that the narrator refers to him as "a ragged gentleman," an "old tattered barrister," and "the old lawyer." (366–367) Similarly, Suttree refers to his uncle John as "John," while the narration consistently refers to him as "the uncle." In this manner, the narration maintains a distance from these two characters. In contrast, the narration will usually refer to Suttree's friends by bizarre nicknames without any description, orientation, or introduction.

The above paragraphs, in combination with the first appendix of this essay, demonstrate that *Suttree* has numerous lapses in a point of view which otherwise remains in the third-person past tense observing Suttree's location. These lapses can often, but not always, be characterized as representing Suttree's thoughts in first, second, and third persons. The narration, however, ultimately has access to information Suttree does not, including entire scenes. In addition, the narrative distance telescopes in a way that makes identifying a narrator difficult, a difficulty exacerbated by the extremely odd style of the narration — nobody in the novel would ever write, speak or think this way.

This is the conclusion of the first half of the essay in which the essay returns to a point made in the fourth paragraph concerning the second epigraph. An alternative paradigm to "narrator" is "narrators." Above, I have demonstrated that the narration can be divided into different voices, which I then attempted to ascribe to the thoughts of characters. But what if we approach this text with the assumption that there are several narrators who trade off frequently? In the example above the example above, in which Gene contemplates a dying rat, perhaps it is one of the narrators who chimes in "it must have been something you ate." Perhaps the entire narration is itself a collage of narrators, some verbose and written, some describing action, some providing colloquialisms such as "he gripped his fork in his fist in the best country manner and fell to." (313) Perhaps each narrator also has its own narrattee, and this is why the implied audience of the book is so difficult to pin down.

This is where the second half of the essay begins. In this half of the essay I will assume that all the above inconsistencies are intended to achieve an effect. This half of the essay describes the effect.

In the last example of inconsistent narrative distance — the way most of the ninety or so characters are typically referred to without introduction as though they were already familiar to all (as compared to the way "the uncle" is introduced again each time he is mentioned and is not allowed to become familiar) — the inconsistency has a consistent effect. In this case, the effect is to contrast Suttree's alienation from lawyer and uncle (his family) to his familiarity with (his friends) Bucket, Gatemouth, J-Bone, Hoghead, Trippin Through the Dew, Ulysses and many other plausibly and implausibly named characters who pass through the novel unintroduced. The narration's inconsistent access also achieves certain effects. One of the effects is that the narrator gives an impression of knowing the story very well. Also, the narrator gives the impression that we know the story well, as though we know all these people and only their names are necessary to bring them to mind. Similarly, it was never necessary to explain Suttree's background — we already know it. It takes only a photo album to bring all those relatives to mind. The mythic quality of the narration also makes the story seem as familiar as a legend. *Suttree* has passed by word of mouth for generations, accumulating embellishments until it become an encyclopedia of every rude joke of the era.

Is this why *Suttree* makes me cry: because it makes me feel as if I lived there? Both the narrative closeups and the absence of introduction bring me into the story. I am oriented to it as though it were my own old memories retold. That is not entirely why it makes me cry. It also has to do with the story I am drawn into.

Suttree lives in a world of drunkenness, poverty, violence, garbage, sewage, and cruel police. He seems strangely content or aimless or both. The fact of his having fallen is all that we know about his fall. His family regards him as a "nasty, vicious person." (19) Immediately before this, this nasty vicious person has just delivered a catfish to a sullen homeless person eating dirty beans and burnt potatoes. Suttree has given up a life of privilege in order to pay attention to people. Suttree can't fight (52, 161), and should be afraid to frequent the neighborhood he does, but he isn't. Suttree is afraid of violence, not people. It is my belief that Suttree doesn't think: a hyperactive narrator ascribes the most ridiculous thoughts to him. Suttree cares about people. But why not his wife and child? Obviously he does care about them: he went to the funeral and cried. As to why he left them? This question is the vacuum at the center of the novel's cyclone. Suttree, his narrators, and his readers all share a collective denial about the bad thing Suttree did. The effect of this is to make me feel that Suttree's background is something we are all trying to avoid thinking about. I think he left them because, as a married father, Suttree would have had to become a character. He would step right into a narrative, until death do them part. His friends would all know his first name. He would have an address, an occupation. His family would bother him and expect him to celebrate holidays. If he ever managed to visit the ragpicker, it would be only to momentarily soothe his aching class consciousness.

Suttree could not be a husband because he is not a character. He has dropped out of narrative. So Suttree drifts. He is a grit of irritation around which no pearl must form. Suttree exists only in the presence of others who like him. Suttree requires a variety of people so that no single impression of him may dominate. When alone with nobody to talk to, the language closes in on him and takes him to someplace strange in his head where his stillborn brother is the only family he ever felt for.

Compare the following two passages offering conspicuous glimpses of Suttree's thoughts at two very different times:

> Imagine a closet, she said.
>
> Imagine.
>
> He got ice from the refrigerator and fixed them drinks and came into the bedroom with them.
>
> Is it five oclock yet? she said.
>
> Of course, said Suttree, clicking the glasses.
>
> She went in to the bathroom and he stood at the window looking out, the drink in his hand. He could see an old man washing at a sink, pale arms and a small paunch hung in his undershirt. Suttree toasted him a mute toast, a shrug of the glass, a gesture indifferent and almost cynical that as he made it caused him something close to shame. (402)

Suttree has it all and has become indifferent. He is rich and bored. He thinks about buying a car. He has a romantic taxiride through snowcovered mountains sipping whiskey with icicles and screwing — and this romantic scene is not entirely touching. After he has walked out of Joyce's story, he resumes drifting:

> At night in the iron bed high in the old house on Grand he'd lie awake and hear the sirens, lonely sound in the city, in the empty streets. He lay in his chrysalis of gloom and made no sound, share by share sharing his pain with those who lay in their blood by the highwayside or in the floors of glass strewn taverns or manacled in jail. He said that even the damned in hell have the community of their suffering and he thought that

he'd guessed out likewise for the living a nominal grief like a grange from which disaster and ruin are proportioned by laws of equity too subtle for divining. (464)

Suttree does not wear a suit and tie of glass but instead wanders naked. He lives in a shack with holes in the wall, riding the currents of Knoxville excrement. He has sunk to the bottom, refusing to be one of those clawing for air. He has left a house too horrifying to name. He is Catholic and has hangups. When they fall at all, they fall directly to hell. So Suttree has forsaken being a character, and he is not what the novel is about.

The novel is about McAnally Flats, death, and the fossils left in limestone where lower creatures died along the muddy riverbanks. It is a historical document recording life in this accidental tidal pool of stagnant culture. It is a scrapbook, a compendium of whiskeytalk. It is the memories nobody lived long enough to have. It is about how America eats his poor. Does the novel, with its dropdead beautiful prose, glorify poverty? Is the novel even about poverty? There is hardly a wealthy person in it. Joyce is the wealthiest character, and she is a criminal. Can a novel be about poverty without displaying the difference and relationship between rich and poor? It is racist, misogynist, and homophobic, but in what ways is it classist?

And why do I find affirmation in it? Is it because I am a white kid who has led a sheltered life and the novel allows me to indulge a sort of voyeurism into poverty without for a second losing my pretensions of erudition through the vehicle of an unobtrusive character whom we only know is a white collegeboy whose life has heretofore been sheltered? Is it because I don't love women, homosexuals, or blacks? It might be because I enjoy novels about alcoholism and heroin addiction. Suttree is not an alcoholic. He shares his last beers (even with Reese who does not share everything he has tucked away). He turns down whiskey (albeit of dubious quality) at least twice. Also, unlike Harvey, he doesn't go visiting relatives in the middle of the night screaming for liquor. Suttree is not an alcoholic, he's just drunk.

Suttree is about love, a flower growing along railroad tracks through whatever miracle renders cinders arable. The novel lavishes every gorgeous word in four centuries of English upon characters who do not expect it. The novel is written to an audience who already knows its stories, but who wants them retold in the loveliest manner possible. It is about Suttree taking the ragpicker and the goatman catfish, about Suttree offering beer to Michael, Gene, Harvey, and buying fishbowls for J-Bone, Hoghead, Bucket, Red, and Cabbage. It is about listening to Daddy Watson's stories, and shaking hands with Trippin Through the Dew. It is about refusing $20 from Clayton and dinner from Aunt Martha. It is about the first cold day of winter, visiting the ragpicker, Gene, and Daddy Watson, making sure they aint froze. It is even about saving the country mouse's life and not letting them cover Red's face until he has finally died. How Suttree found his own corpse in bed. It is about condoms like leeches, fish like dogs, rats like beetles, lice like lizards, hogs like quail, flies like cats, rats like cats, and cats like cats.

APPENDIX ONE
INDEX OF SCENES

pages	description	time	point of view
3–5	inexplicable intro		
(page break)			
7–29	corpse, Ragman, John	Summer, Sunday, 1951	drift 13–14, 27–29
30–31	washing	August, 1950	Gene's sister
31–32	melons		Gene
32–33	melons again		Brogans (farmer)
33–34	about melons		2 Brogans (farmers)
34–35	melons, shotgun		drift: Gene / farmers
36–44	Gene into prison		Gene

44–48	prison morning		
48–54	goddamn tapping	Autumn, 1950	Suttree
54–60	julep		
60–62	mother, release	Winter, 1950	
63–80	Sut begins drinking.	Summer, Monday, 1951	
80–86	Hangover, jail	Summer, Tuesday, 1951	
87–90	Daddy Watson	at least a week later (87, 109)	
91–106	junkman, railroader, ragpicker, Jake		Gene
107–112	Ab Jones, Howard Clevinger's	(happens simultaneously with the previous scene)	Suttree
112–113	Ab Jones		
113–116	Gene arrives		
116–118	viaduct		Gene

119–125	baptism	Summer, Sunday, 1951	Suttree
125–136	Aunt Martha, mansion		
137–143	pig	Summer, 1951	Gene
143–147	work	Autumn, 1951	drift: Gene, Sut, Trippin, Mother She, shutin, ragman
148–150	dead son		Suttree
150–152	mother-in-law		
152–161	funeral, Stanton, kid		
162–176	the general	Thanksgiving, 1951	
176–179	trolley		
180–182	Daddy Watson	Winter, 1951–1952	
183–184	waiting for 5 AM beer		
184	Suttree wakes		

184–192	riot, hospital	(same day as 183)	
192–194	Daddy Watson		
195–205	goatman, Ab Jones	Spring, 1952	drift: goatman, Suttree
205–206	goatman's catfish		Suttree
207–210	bats		Gene
210–212	boat		
212–213	pharmacist		
213–214	Listen, Sut		
214–217	bats		Gene, Suttree, Gene
217–219	$1.25		
219	caves		
220–227	Michael, Ab Jones		Suttree

227–234	Mother She, Michael		
234–237	Comer's, Leonard		
237–240	Michael, turtle soup		
241–245	weird Leonard		
245–252	girl, weird Leonard		
253–255	church		
256–257	trash		Ragpicker
257–258	God		Ragpicker / Suttree
259	fallen truck		Gene
259–260	maps		
260–262	hole		
262–263	Dynamite, he said		

263–264	Gene, you're crazy		Gene / Suttree
264–268	Clifford		Junkman
268–269	concussion		Suttree
269–270	explosion		Gene
270–274	dog		Suttree
274–275	darkness		Gene
275–277	rescue		Suttree
278–282	Mother She, Ab Jones		
282	Mother She		Suttree, drift
283–291	mountain	Late October, 1952	Suttree
291–295	Bryson City, S. C.		
295–297	Mrs. Long's house		

298–302	$300	3 December 1952	
302–305	$100		
306–313	Reese	Spring 1953	
313–315	Reese's wife		Gene
315–316	them		Gene / Suttree
316–331	musslin'		Suttree
331–347	Newport, Tennessee		
347–348	back at camp		
348–353	Wanda		
353	Wanda		
353–356	Wanda		
356–357 Willard		third week August, 1953	

357–358	Wanda		
358–363	Wanda's death		
363	He left		
364–366	Ragpicker		
366	orchard		
366–368	Dr Neal, old man, dog		
368–371	Blind Richard, tabletop		
371–372	Reese		
372–373	÷ $70, Blind Richard		
374–378	death of Red		drift, Suttree
379–385	burning house	Winter, 1953	Suttree
385–390	Joyce		

390–401	Joyce, $500		
401–402	Joyce, $1100		
402–403	death of Hoghead	February, 1954	
403–404	Michael		
404–405	Joyce, -$500	early May, 1954	
405–411	Joyce, -$1850		
411–415	lamp	October, 1954	
416–420	Weird Leonard		
421–422	death of the Rag-picker		
423–427	She, hallucination		
427–430	hallucination		
431–434	Aunt Alice		

435–438	trouble		Gene
438–439	Gene imprisoned		
440–442	Ab Jones, police car		Suttree
442–443	Ab Jones		Ab Jones
443	Tarzan Quinn		drift
443–444	Doll		Suttree
444–446	room		
446–447	death of Ab Jones		
448–464	Typhoid fever		
465–467	death of Suttree, Josie		
467–469	Trippin Through Dew		
469–470	Old Suttree aint dead		

470–471	Fly Them		

Appendix Two
Select Index of Characters

author

William Gillespie has published 14 and 5/6 books of his fiction and poetry under six different names.

ACKNOWLEDGEMENTS

It is rare, in my experience, to get as deeply into a book as I am into *Suttree*, and to then find other people traversing that wild interior. I am eternally grateful to the folks who took an interest in this essay.

Sure Do Wish You'd Get Ye One of These Here Taters written by William Gillespie.

SBPB4B.
12 September MMXXV.
ISBN: 978-0-9853578-7-0
$14.

Spineless Books
PO Box 91
Urbana, IL
61801
USA

SPINELESS

BOOKS

Founded 20-02-2002, Spineless Books is an independent literary publishing house dedicated to the production and distribution of innovative literature, in print and electronic form, with an emphasis on collaborative writing, formal experimentation, and utopian thought.

Secretary, Editor: Dirk Stratton
Literature Facilitator: William Gillespie

"Advice to struggling writers: Stop struggling and write"—Junetta Gillespie

SPINELESS BOOKS | URBANA, IL

FLY THEM.

www.ingramcontent.com/pod-product-compliance
Lightning Source LLC
Chambersburg PA
CBHW050907180626
46814CB00007B/2930